Pebble® Plus

Happy Birthday!

Birthday Customs around the World

by Sarah L. Schuette

Consulting editor: Gail Saunders-Smith, PhD

CAPSTONE PRESS

a capstone imprint

Pebble Plus is published by Capstone Press,
151 Good Counsel Drive, P.O. Box 669, Mankato, Minnesota 56002.
www.capstonepress.com

092009
005618CGS10

 Books published by Capstone Press are manufactured with paper
containing at least 10 percent post-consumer waste.

Library of Congress Cataloging-in-Publication Data
Schuette, Sarah L., 1976–
      Birthday customs around the world / by Sarah L. Schuette.
       p. cm. — (Pebble plus. happy birthday!)
      Includes bibliographical references and index.
      Summary: "Simple text and colorful photographs describe birthday traditions in different countries" — Provided
by publisher.
      ISBN 978-1-4296-4001-5 (library binding)
      1. Birthdays — Juvenile literature. I. Title.
GT2430.S38 2010
394.2 — dc22   2009026273

Editorial credits
Erika L. Shores, editor; Ashlee Suker, designer; Wanda Winch, media researcher; Eric Manske, production specialist;
      Sarah Schuette, photo stylist; Marcy Morin, scheduler

Photo credits
Capstone Studio/Karon Dubke, 1, 5, 7, 11, 13, 15, 19, 21
Index Stock Imagery/MIXA Co. Ltd., 17
Peter Arnold/Sean Sprague, cover, 9

The Capstone Press Photo Studio thanks Countryside Homes, in Mankato, Minn., for their help with photo
      shoots for this book.

The author dedicates this book to her father, Willmar Schuette, for always making her birthday special.

Note to Parents and Teachers

The Happy Birthday! set supports national social studies standards related to culture. This book
describes and illustrates birthday customs around the world. The images support early readers
in understanding the text. The repetition of words and phrases helps early readers learn new
words. This book also introduces early readers to subject-specific vocabulary words, which are
defined in the Glossary section. Early readers may need assistance to read some words and to
use the Table of Contents, Glossary, Read More, Internet Sites, and Index sections of the book.

Table of Contents

Birthday Customs

Everyone has a birthday. What customs do people celebrate around the world on their birthdays?

Birthday Food

People eat special food
on their birthdays.
Pancakes with fruit
are a birthday treat
in the Netherlands.

Mei eats long noodles

on her birthday.

She lives in China.

Having Fun

People everywhere have fun
on their birthdays.
In Mexico, Papan grabs
candy that falls out
of a piñata.

Vera gets six pulls
on her earlobe to mark
her sixth birthday.
She lives in Brazil.

Sam gets butter on his nose
for his birthday.
Some people in Canada
butter noses for good luck.

Jimi lives in Japan.

He wears new clothes
on his birthday.

Macey has a birthday party

in Australia.

Everyone claps six times

for her six years.

Your Birthday

Where do you live?

How do you celebrate

your birthday?

Glossary

celebrate — to do something fun to mark a special event such as a birthday

custom — a special way of doing something

earlobe — the part of your outer ear that hangs down

piñata — a decorated box that is filled with candy and gifts; piñatas are broken with sticks or bats.

Read More

Lieberman, Channah. *Happy Birthday to Me!* Brooklyn: Hachai, 2006.

Powell, Jillian. *A Birthday.* Why Is This Day Special? North Mankato, Minn.: Smart Apple Media, 2007.

Rustad, Martha E. H. *Birthdays in Many Cultures.* Life around the World. Mankato, Minn.: Capstone Press, 2009.

Internet Sites

FactHound offers a safe, fun way to find Internet sites related to this book. All of the sites on FactHound have been researched by our staff.

Here's all you do:

Visit *www.facthound.com*

FactHound will fetch the best sites for you!

Index

Word Count: 131

Grade: 1

Early-Intervention Level: 18